ANOTHER FOOT AT A TIME

30 popular pieces arranged for manuals and up to six pedal notes

COLIN HAND

First published in Great Britain in 1999 by Kevin Mayhew Ltd
Buxhall, Stowmarket, Suffolk IP14 3BW
Tel: +44 (0) 1449 737978 Fax: +44 (0) 1449 737834
E-mail: info@kevinmayhewltd.com

www.kevinmayhew.com

© Copyright 1999 Kevin Mayhew Ltd.

The music in this book is protected by copyright and may not be reproduced
in any way for sale or private use without the consent of the copyright owner.

Front cover photograph of the organ at St Peter and St Paul, Bromley,
by J. W. Thomas. Reproduced by kind permission of J. W. Walker & Sons Ltd.,
Organ Makers.

Illustrations by Graham Johnstone. Reproduced by kind permission of
P & S Organ Supply Company Ltd.

ISBN 978 1 84003 445 9
ISMN M 57004 603 4
Catalogue No. 1400215

Cover design: Jaquetta Sergeant
Music setting: Andrew Moore
Proofreader: Rachel Judd

Printed and bound in Great Britain

Contents

Two Manuals and Three Pedals

i) Solo and accompaniment

		Page
On Wings of Song	Mendelssohn	7
Serenade	Haydn	10
Hungarian Dance No. 5	Brahms	14
Largo from 'New World Symphony'	Dvořák	17

ii) Changing manuals

Two Rondos	Susato	20
Waltz in A	Schubert	22
See, The Conquering Hero Comes from 'Judas Maccabaeus'	Handel	24
Rondo from Sonatina No. 1	Pleyel	27
The Heavens Are Telling from 'The Creation'	Haydn	30

Four Pedals

i) Solo and accompaniment

Berceuse from 'Dolly Suite'	Fauré	34
Morning from 'Peer Gynt'	Grieg	37
Gymnopédie I	Satie	40
Minuet	Boccherini	42

ii) Manual and registration changes

Symphony and Chorus from 'Come, ye Sons of Art'	Purcell	45
Minuet in G	Bach	48
Hornpipe from the 'Water Music'	Handel	50
Chorus from 'The Merry Wives of Windsor'	Nicolai	53

Four Pedals - More Advanced

		Page
Minuet from 'Samson'	Handel	56
Papageno's Aria from 'The Magic Flute'	Mozart	60
Prelude from 'Te Deum'	Charpentier	62
Radetsky March	Strauss	66
Humoreske No. 7	Dvořák	70
Courante from 'Choice lessons'	Greene	72

Five Pedals In Two Groups

Melody in F	Rubinstein	74
Dance-duet from 'Hansel and Gretel'	Humperdinck	77
Alleluia from 'Exultate Jubilate'	Mozart	80

Six Pedals In Two Groups

Meditation from 'Thaïs'	Massenet	84
Largo from 'Xerxes'	Handel	87
Venetian Gondola Song	Mendelssohn	90
Dance of the Blessed Spirits from 'Orpheus'	Gluck	93

Foreword

This book, like its predecessor, *One Foot at a Time*, has been compiled to provide a starting point for those pianists who have been cajoled or press-ganged into playing the organ for their local church services. These so-called 'reluctant organists', of which there are many, deserve our admiration. To be expected to play in public, confronted by an instrument with two or three keyboards, a pedal-board, an array of enigmatically named stops and perhaps several pistons and lever controls, is daunting to say the least. This collection is therefore offered as a continuation of the step-by-step guide to organ management of the previous book.

The collection presumes only a moderate ability on the piano and includes well-known pieces from the classical repertoire which will provide not only pleasure in practice but ready-made voluntaries for church use.

Most organs have two or three keyboards, or 'manuals', and a pedal-board. On a two-manual instrument the upper one is known as the Swell (Sw.) and the lower one the Great (Gt.). A third manual, the Choir (Ch.), is usually situated below the Great. The *written* compass of each manual extends from low C (two octaves below middle C) upwards for about 4 ¾ octaves, whilst the pedal-board ranges from that same C upwards for about 2 ½ octaves to F or G. Although the compass of the manuals is less than that of the piano, the overall range of available sounds is much wider. The sounds are controlled by drawstops sited on side panels and labelled with the name of the manual to which each applies. (Some modern organs have rows of ivory coloured rocking tablets in lieu of drawstops.)

Each manual stop (*fig. 1*) has a name (Diapason, Principal, Flute, etc.) together with a number (8', 4' or 2'). When drawn, all 8' stops will produce notes at the same pitch as the written ones (as on the piano), while 4' and 2' stops produce notes an octave and two octaves higher respectively. The pedal stops are also named (Bourdon, Bass Flute, etc.) and carry numbers (8', 16' and, on large instruments, 32'). A pedal note depressed with an 8' stop drawn will produce notes sounding as written, while 16' and 32' stops produce notes an octave and two octaves lower respectively. The basic sound of the manuals is 8' pitch and that of the pedals 16', these stops being the most frequently used.

Apart from the stops which control the actual sound from the pipes, there are others called couplers which, when drawn, link up manuals and pedals so that notes played on one keyboard will cause the same notes to sound on another. The most commonly used couplers link the Swell to the Great and the pedals to one or other of the manuals.

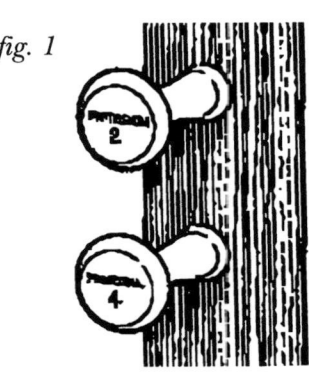

fig. 1

The orthodox method of building up organ tone from very soft to very loud is to begin with the softest 8' stop to which other 8' stops are added in order of loudness. The 4' stops come next (adding an octave above) and then the 2' stops for brightness. Finally the Reeds (Tromba, Horn, etc.) will complete the picture.

Present-day pedal technique employs both the toe and heel of each foot. The signs **v** and **o** above the bass notes indicate that they should be played with the right toe and heel respectively while **ʌ** and **o** under the bass notes refer to the left toe and heel. The pedal notes should be depressed by movement from the ankle rather than from the knee.

The first three groups of pieces in this collection have been so arranged that each piece calls for the use of only two pedals to each foot as in the last group in the pevious book, thus establishing a sound technique and giving the player early confidence. In addition, however, these pieces provide practice in manual and stop changes. The last two groups of pieces involve the use of three adjacent pedals to each foot. In these instances the middle one can be regarded as a pivot (without depressing it) so that by turning the ankle to the right or left, the toe or heel can easily find the pedal note above or below.

The pipes operated from the Swell manual are enclosed in a box that has movable shutters similar to Venetian blinds. These are controlled by a balanced pivoting Swell pedal placed centrally or to the right above the pedal board (*fig. 2*). With the right foot placed firmly

fig. 2

and squarely on this pedal, the player can produce a crescendo and decrescendo by pressure on the toe and heel respectively which opens and closes the shutters of the Swell box. Well-controlled movement is required to produce even graduations of tone, particularly at the beginning of a crescendo. Some older organs have a notched lever Swell pedal which, unlike the balanced one, cannot be left partly open.

Most organs have some mechanical means for moving stops in and out, thus enabling the player's hands to remain in contact with the keyboard. These devices usually come in the form of button-shaped thumb-operated pistons situated under each manual (*fig. 3*), and foot levers (known as composition pedals) projecting above the pedal-board (*fig. 2*). These pistons and levers will draw and cancel stops, enabling swift volume changes to be made. One of the most useful of these devices is that which can draw or cancel the Great to Pedal coupler.

fig. 3

To conclude, it must be said that organs differ widely in construction and layout, and even similarly named stops can vary in quality and sound from one instrument to another. Players should therefore feel free to experiment when practising in order to discover the most effective and useful combinations of stops on their own particular instrument. After all, it is the sound that matters most and even when every bit of advice has been dispensed, the ear is the final arbiter.

ON WINGS OF SONG

Felix Mendelssohn (1809-1847)

© Copyright 1999 Kevin Mayhew Ltd.
It is illegal to photocopy music.

SERENADE

Franz Joseph Haydn (1732-1809)

Solo (or Gt.) 8' **mp** ; Sw. 8' **p** ; Ped. 16' **p**
Sw. to Ped.; Sw. to Solo (or Gt.)

Andante cantabile

* *Avoid playing through rests*

© Copyright 1999 Kevin Mayhew Ltd.
It is illegal to photocopy music.

HUNGARIAN DANCE No. 5

Johannes Brahms (1833-1897)

Gt. 8' Solo (Reed) *mf*-*f* ; Sw. 8' *mf*-*f* ; Ped. 16'
Sw. to Ped. (Sw. to Gt. ad lib.)

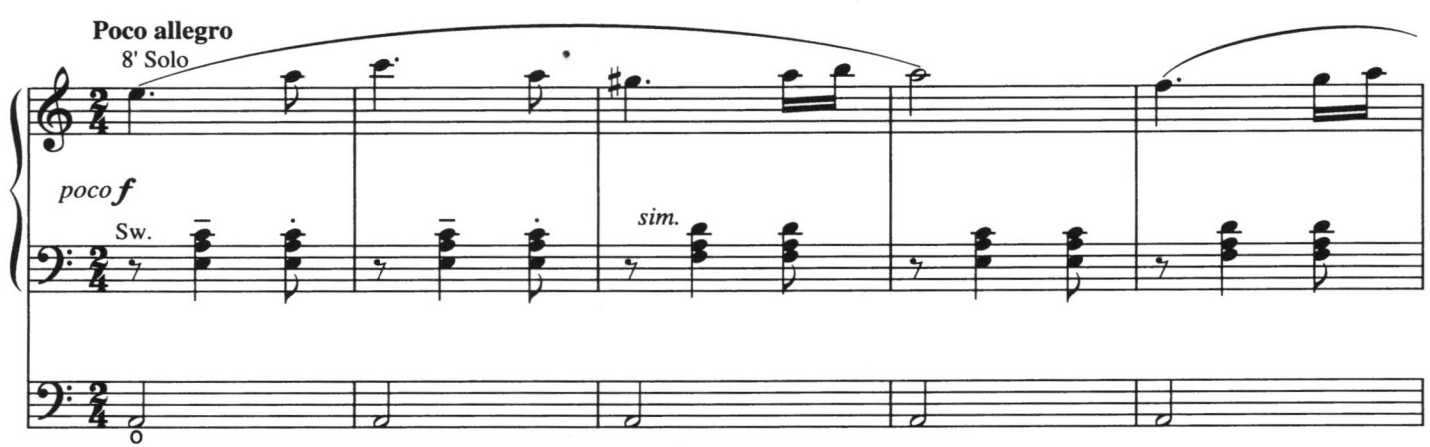

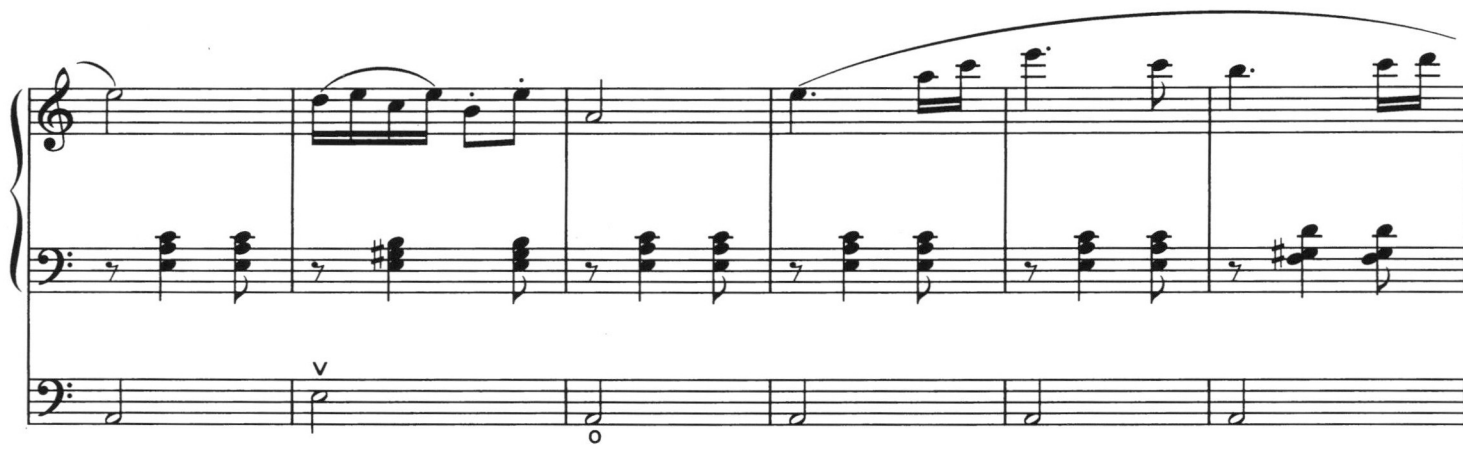

LARGO from 'NEW WORLD SYMPHONY'

Antonín Dvorák (1841-1904)

Sw. 8' Reed *p*
Ch. or Gt. 8' *p*
Ped. 16'
Ch. or Gt. to Ped.

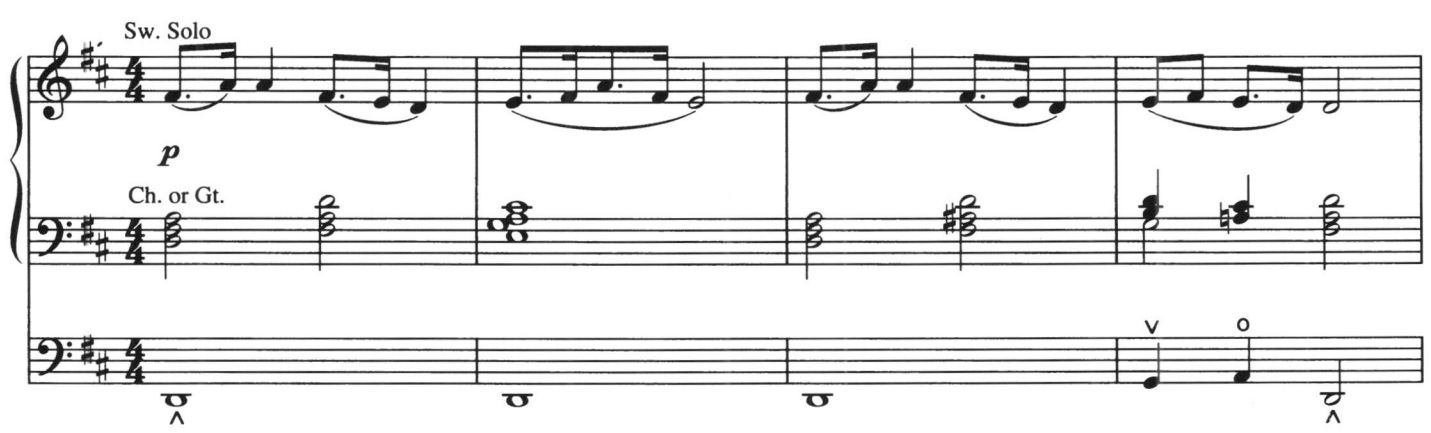

* Open swell box very gradually

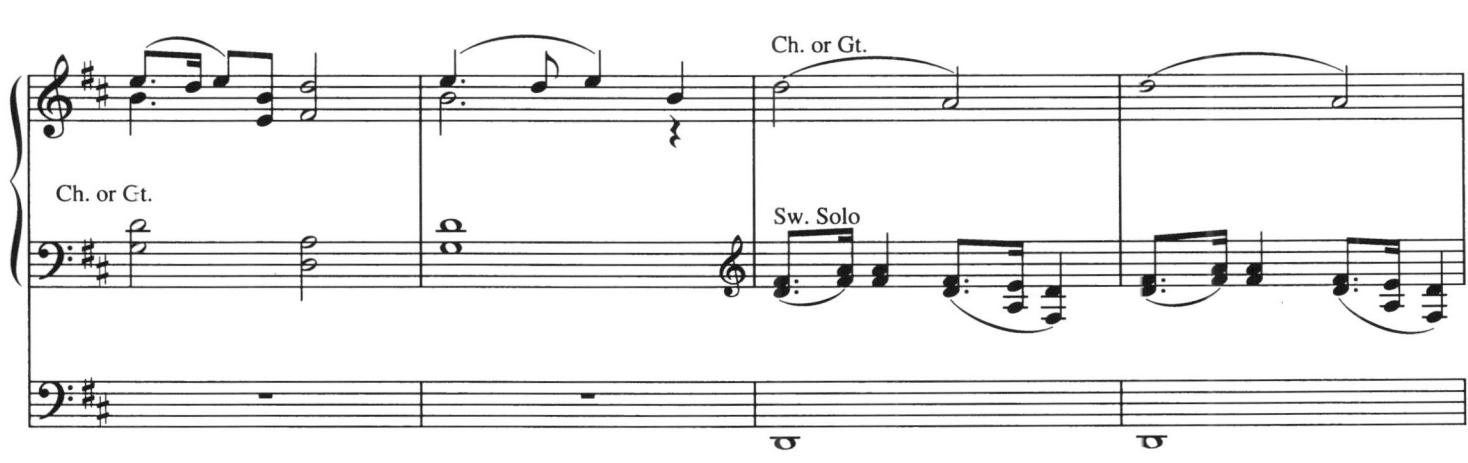

19

TWO RONDOS

Tylman Susato (c.1500-c.1561)

Sw. 8' 4' *mp*
Gt. 8' 4' *mf*
Ped. 16' 8'
Sw. to Ped.

Fine

© Copyright 1999 Kevin Mayhew Ltd.
It is illegal to photocopy music.

WALTZ in A

Franz Schubert (1797-1828)

Sw. 8' 4' *mf*; Gt. 8' 4' *f*; Ped. 16'
Sw. to Gt.; Sw. to Ped.

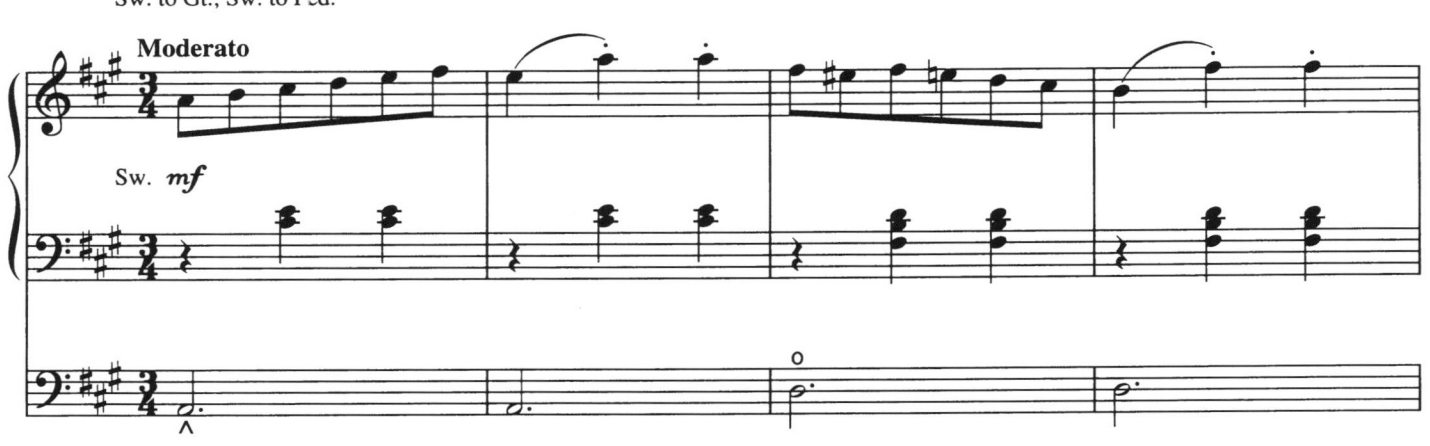

© Copyright 1999 Kevin Mayhew Ltd.
It is illegal to photocopy music.

*Add 2' to Gt. if possible.

SEE, THE CONQUERING HERO COMES
from 'JUDAS MACCABAEUS'

George Frideric Handel (1685-1759)

Sw. 8' 4' *mf*; Gt. 8' 4' *f*; Ped. 16' 8'
Sw. to Gt.; Sw. to Ped.

© Copyright 1999 Kevin Mayhew Ltd.
It is illegal to photocopy music.

RONDO from SONATINA No. 1

Ignaz Joseph Pleyel (1757-1831)

THE HEAVENS ARE TELLING from 'THE CREATION'

Franz Joseph Haydn (1732-1809)

Sw. 8' 4' *mf* ; Gt. 8' 4' 2' *f* ; (Ch. 8' *mp*) ; Ped. 16' 8'
Sw. to Ped.
Gt. to Ped.

© Copyright 1999 Kevin Mayhew Ltd.
It is illegal to photocopy music.

BERCEUSE from 'DOLLY SUITE'

Gabriel Fauré (1845-1924)

MORNING from 'PEER GYNT'

Edvard Grieg (1843-1907)

Ch. or Gt. 8' solo *p* ; Sw. 8' *p* ; Gt. 16'
Sw. to Ped.

Allegretto

Solo Ch. or Gt.

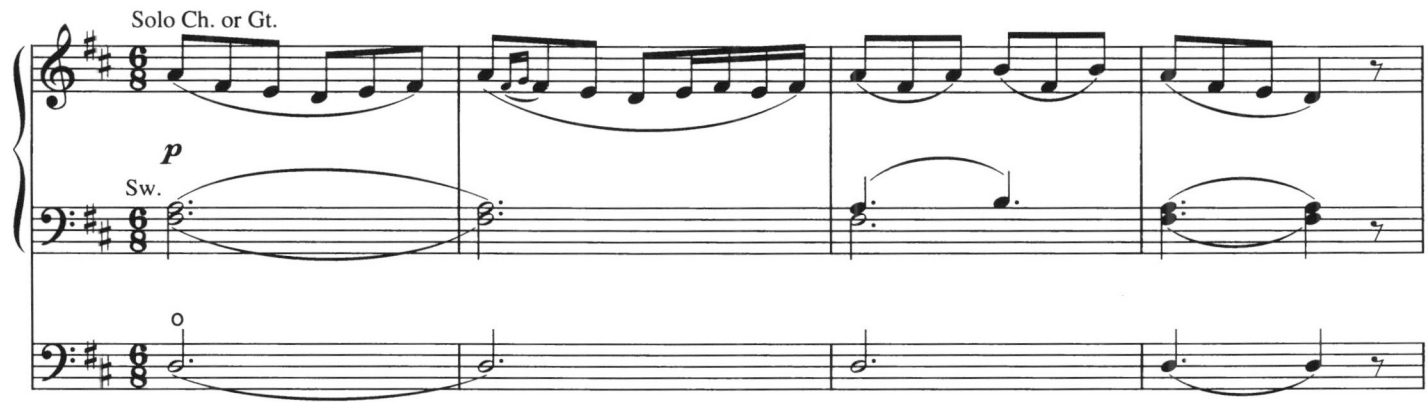

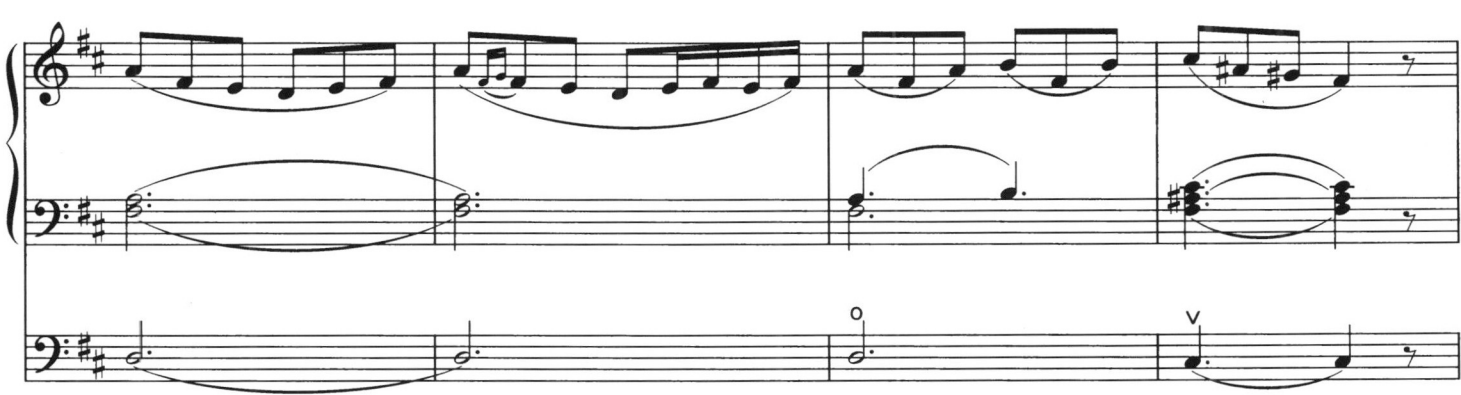

© Copyright 1999 Kevin Mayhew Ltd.
It is illegal to photocopy music.

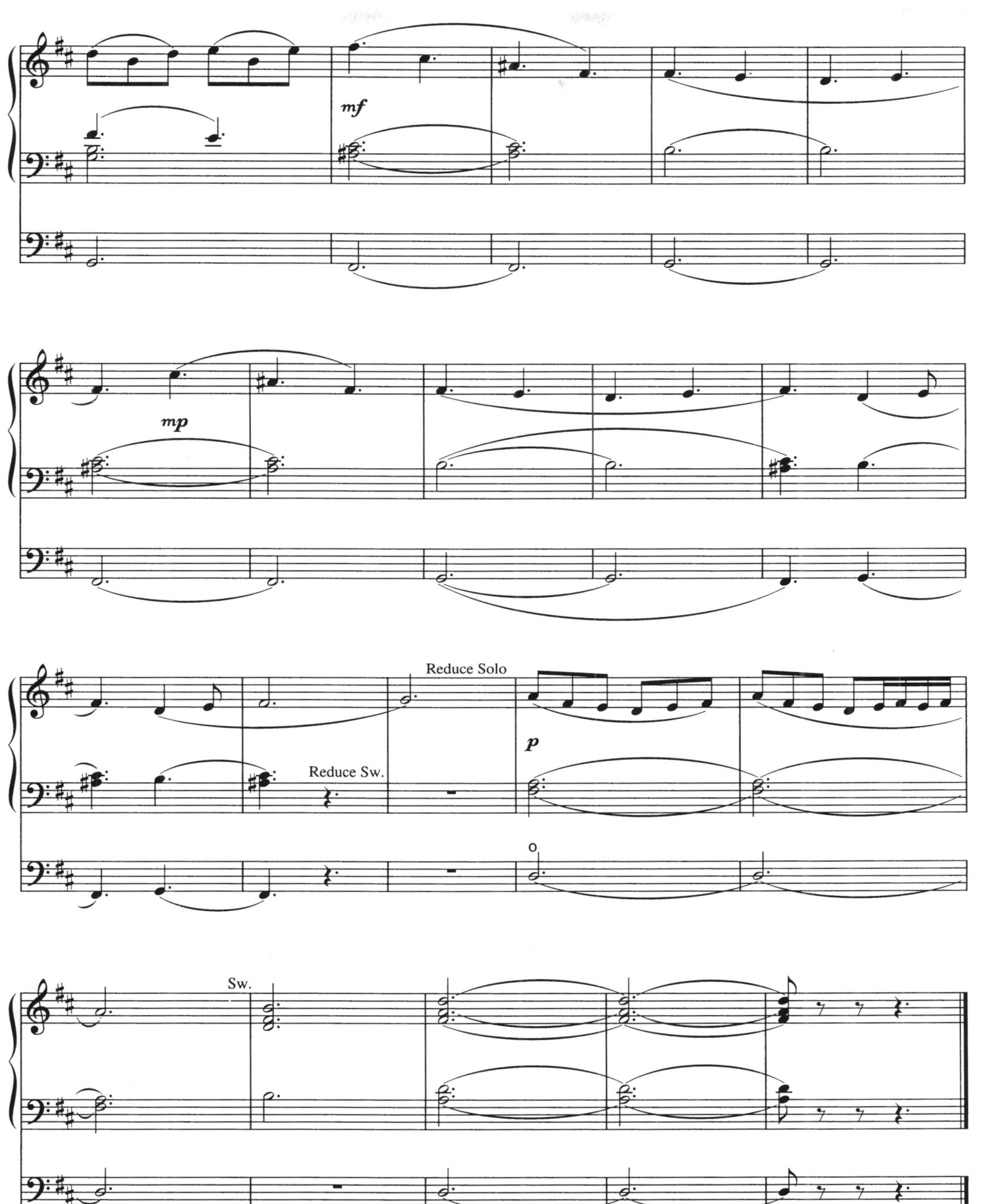

GYMNOPEDIE No. I

Erik Satie (1866-1925)

Gt./Ch. 8' *p*
Sw. 8' *pp*
Ped. 16' *pp*
Sw. to Ped.

MINUET

Luigi Boccherini (1743-1805)

Gt. 8' *mp* ; Sw. 8' *mp* ; Ped. 16'
Sw. to Ped.

© Copyright 1999 Kevin Mayhew Ltd.
It is illegal to photocopy music.

SYMPHONY and CHORUS
from 'COME, YE SONS OF ART'

Henry Purcell (1659-1695)

MINUET in G

Johann Sebastian Bach (1685-1750)

Gt. 8' 4' **mf** ; Sw. 8' 4' **mp** ; Ped. 16'
Sw. to Gt.; Sw. to Ped.

HORNPIPE from the 'WATER MUSIC'

George Frideric Handel (1685-1759)

Gt. 8' 4' *f*
Solo Trumpet or Tuba*
Ped. 16'
Gt. to Ped.

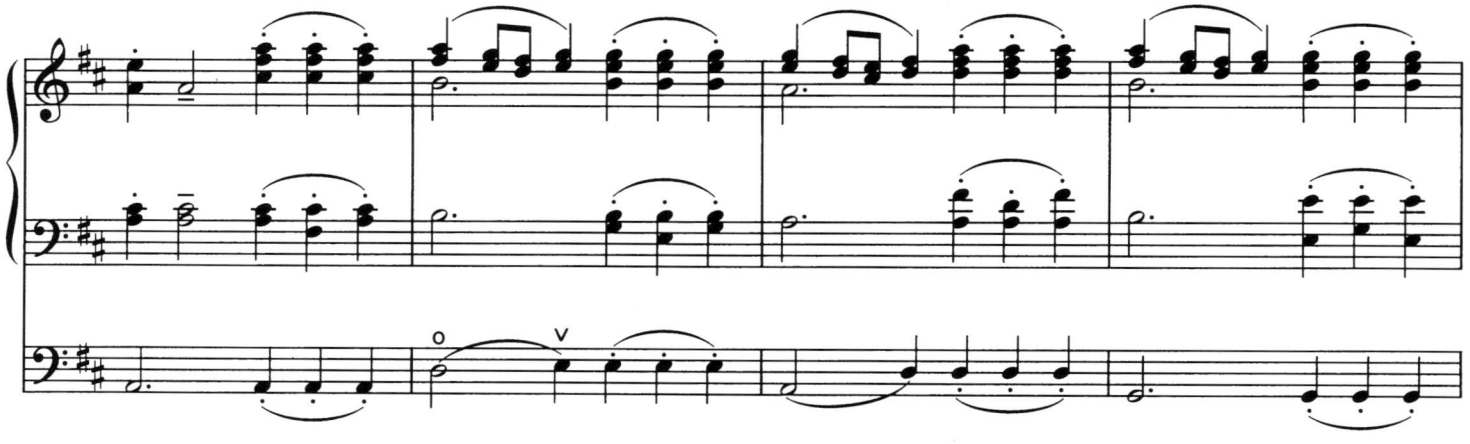

** In the absence of a solo Trumpet, use Sw. 8' 4' in lieu of Gt. and play
solo Trumpet on Gt. using prominent 8' stops and Reeds, if available.*

© Copyright 1999 Kevin Mayhew Ltd.
It is illegal to photocopy music.

CHORUS from
'THE MERRY WIVES OF WINDSOR'

Otto Nicolai (1810-1849)

Sw. 8' 4' **mf**; Gt. 8' 4' 2' **f**; Ped. 16' 8'
Sw. to Gt.; Sw. to Ped.

Allegro

Add 2' to Sw. for repeat

© Copyright 1999 Kevin Mayhew Ltd.
It is illegal to photocopy music.

*Reposition right heel on C

MINUET from 'SAMSON'

George Frideric Handel (1685-1759)

Sw. 8' 4' *mp* ; Gt. 8' 4' *mf* ; Ped. 16'
Sw. to Gt.; Sw. to Ped.; Gt. to Ped.

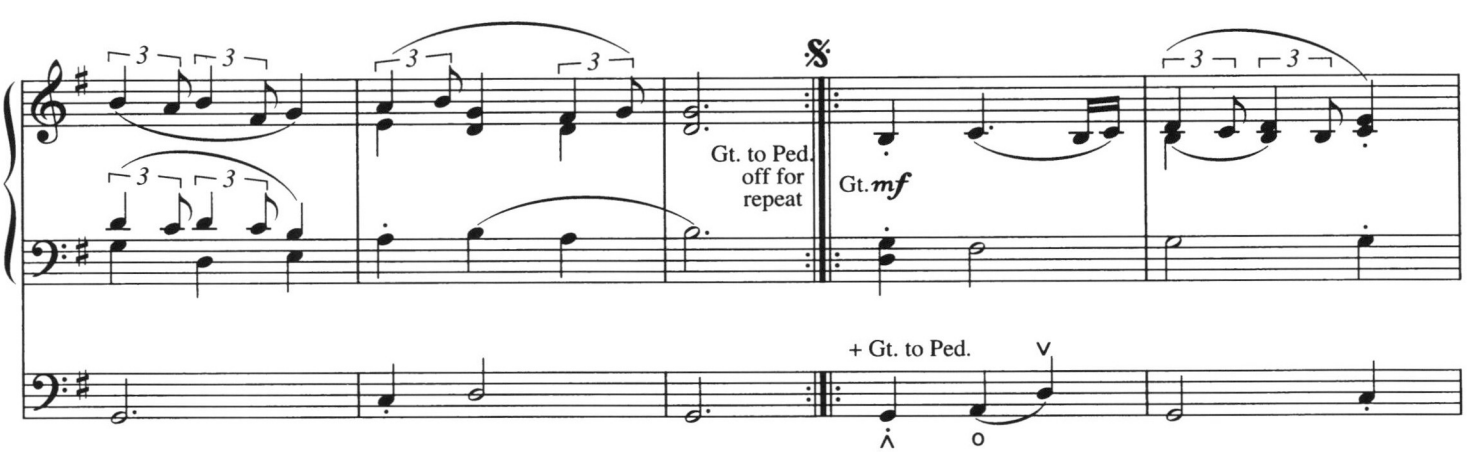

© Copyright 1999 Kevin Mayhew Ltd.
It is illegal to photocopy music.

PAPAGENO'S ARIA from 'THE MAGIC FLUTE'

Wolfgang Amadeus Mozart (1756-1791)

Gt. 8' 4' **mf**
Sw. 8' 4' **mp**
Ped. 16'
Sw. to Gt.
Sw. to Ped.

© Copyright 1999 Kevin Mayhew Ltd.
It is illegal to photocopy music.

PRELUDE from 'TE DEUM'

Marc-Antoine Charpentier (1634-1704)

Trumpet or Solo Reed 8' *f* *
Gt. 8' 4' *f*
Ped. 16' 8'
Gt. to Ped.

Allegro marziale

* In the absence of a Trumpet or Solo Reed, use Gt. 8' stops
  for solo line and Sw. (with Sw. to Ped.) in lieu of Gt.

© Copyright 1999 Kevin Mayhew Ltd.
It is illegal to photocopy music.

RADETSKY MARCH

Johann Strauss (1804-1849)

Gt. 8' 4' 2' **f**; Sw. 8' 4' **mp**; Ch. 8' **p**; Ped. 16' 8'
Sw. to Gt.; Sw. to Ped.; Gt. to Ped.

* *Avoid playing through the rests in the pedal part*

© Copyright 1999 Kevin Mayhew Ltd.
It is illegal to photocopy music.

HUMORESKE No. 7

Antonín Dvořák (1841-1904)

Solo (Gt. or Ch.) 8' **mp**
Sw. 8' **mp**
Ped. 16'
Sw. to Ped.

Andante
Solo 8'

* *Use right foot on Swell pedal*
** *Reposition right foot over C/D*

© Copyright 1999 Kevin Mayhew Ltd.
It is illegal to photocopy music.

** *Reposition right foot over C/D*

COURANTE from 'CHOICE LESSONS'

Maurice Greene (1695-1755)

Sw. 8' 4' 2' *f*
Gt. 8' 4' 2' *ff*
Ped. 16' 8'
Sw. to Gt.
Gt. to Ped.

Poco Allegro

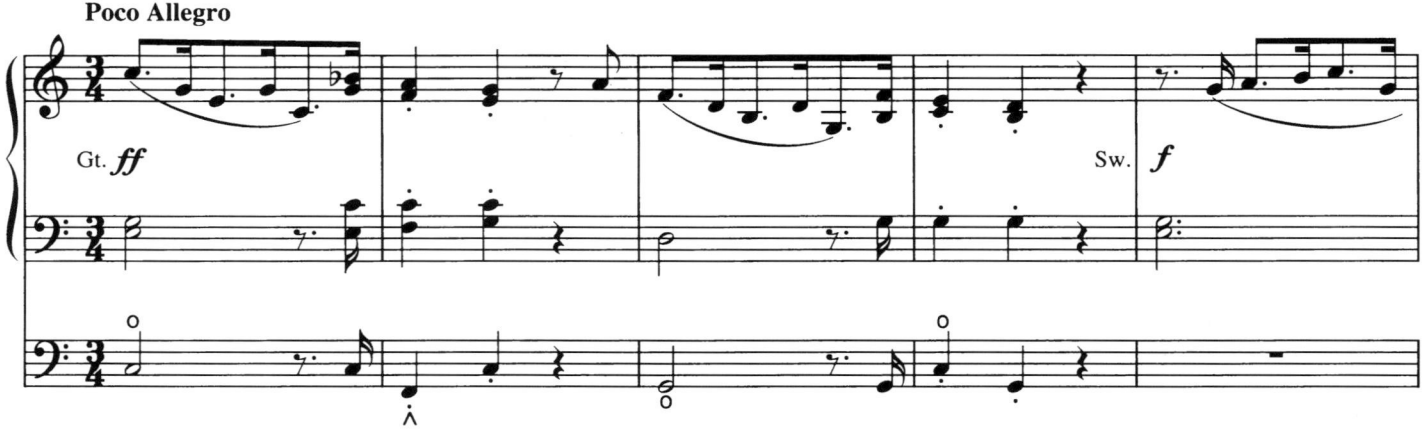

* *Reposition right foot over C/D after using Swell crescendo pedal.*

© Copyright 1999 Kevin Mayhew Ltd.
It is illegal to photocopy music.

MELODY IN F

Anton Rubinstein (1829-1894)

Gt. or Ch. Solo 8' *mp*
Sw. 8' *p* ; Ped. 16'
Sw. to Ped.

Moderato

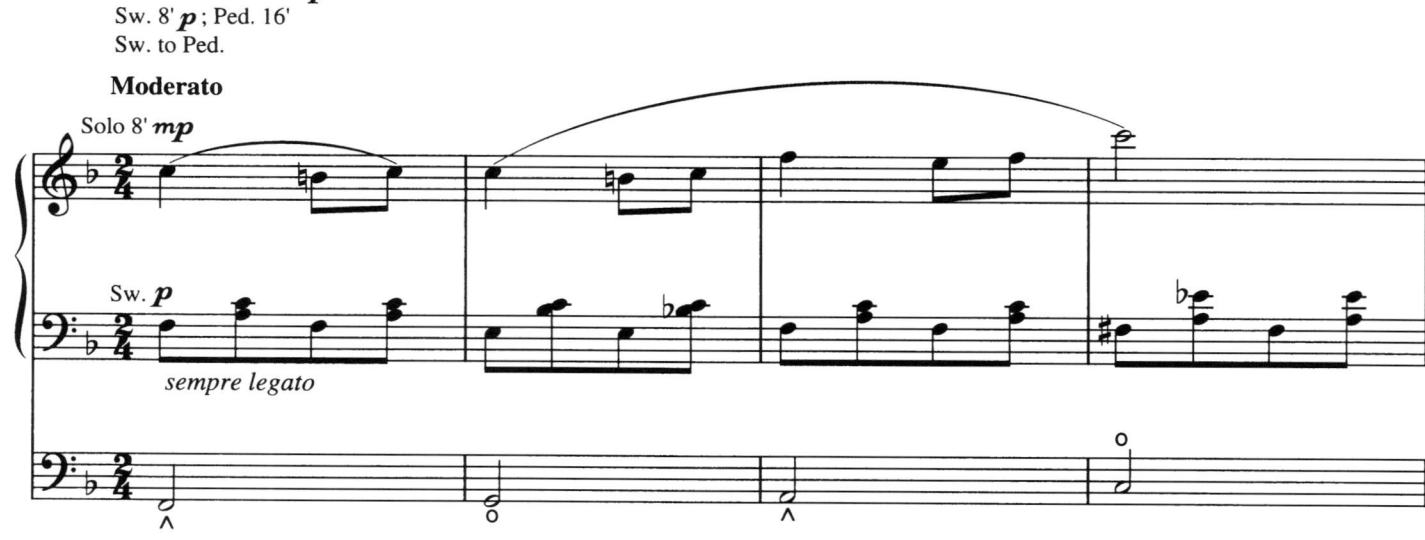

© Copyright 1999 Kevin Mayhew Ltd.
It is illegal to photocopy music.

DANCE-DUET from 'HANSEL AND GRETEL'

Engelbert Humperdinck (1854-1921)

Sw. 8' 4' *mp*
Gt. 8' 4' *mf*
Ped. 16'
Sw. to Ped.
Sw. to Gt.

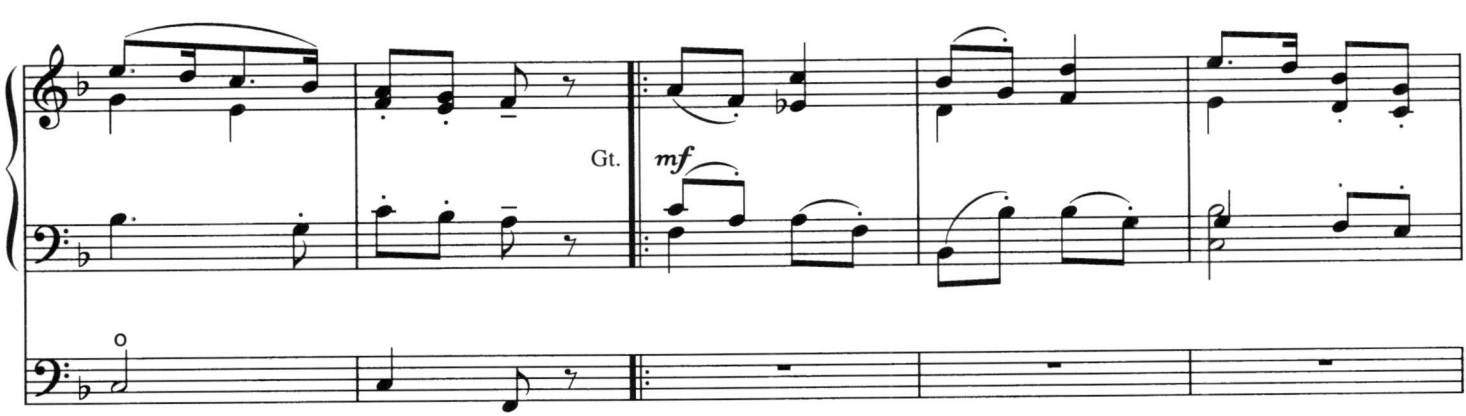

© Copyright 1999 Kevin Mayhew Ltd.
It is illegal to photocopy music.

ALLELUIA from 'EXULTATE JUBILATE'

Wolfgang Amadeus Mozart (1756-1791)

Sw. 8' 4' *mp* Sw. to Gt.
Gt. 8' 4' *mf* Sw. to Ped.
Ped. 16' Gt. to Ped.

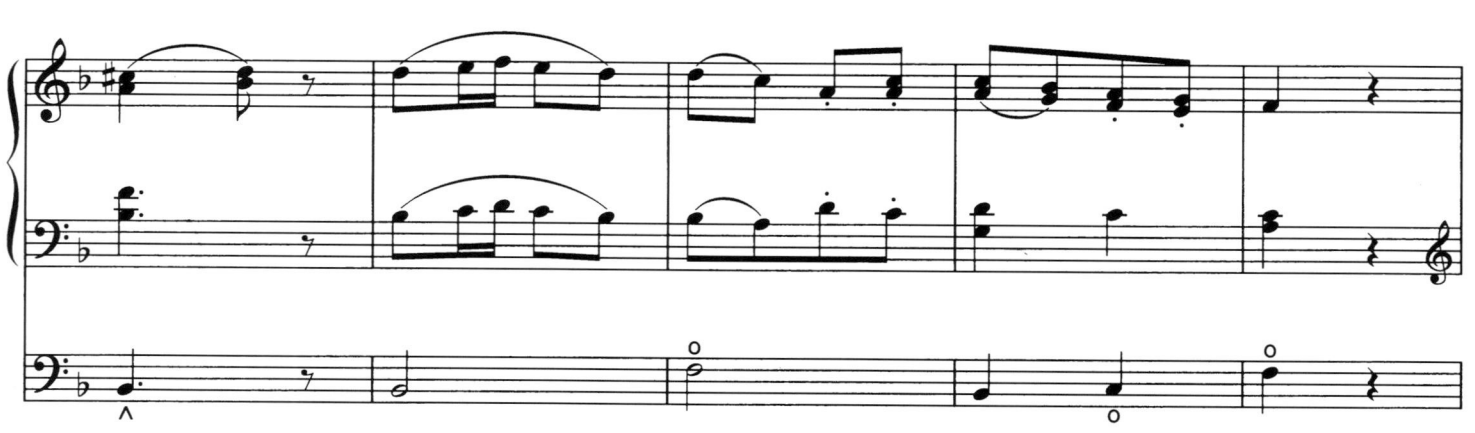

© Copyright 1999 Kevin Mayhew Ltd.
It is illegal to photocopy music.

MEDITATION from 'THAÏS'

Jules Massenet (1842-1912)

Solo (Gt. or Ch.) 8' *mp*
Sw. 8' *mp*
Ped. 16'
Sw. to Ped.

Initially, position the right heel over middle D and the left heel over low A.
Use these positions as pivots to play middle E and C with the right toe,
and low G and B with the left toe.

© Copyright 1999 Kevin Mayhew Ltd.
It is illegal to photocopy music.

85

LARGO from 'XERXES'

George Frideric Handel (1685-1759)

* 'Pivot' left heel on A without depressing it.

89

VENETIAN GONDOLA SONG

Felix Mendelssohn (1809-1847)

Solo (or Gt.) 8' **mp**
Sw. 8' **p**
Ped. 16'
Sw. to Ped.

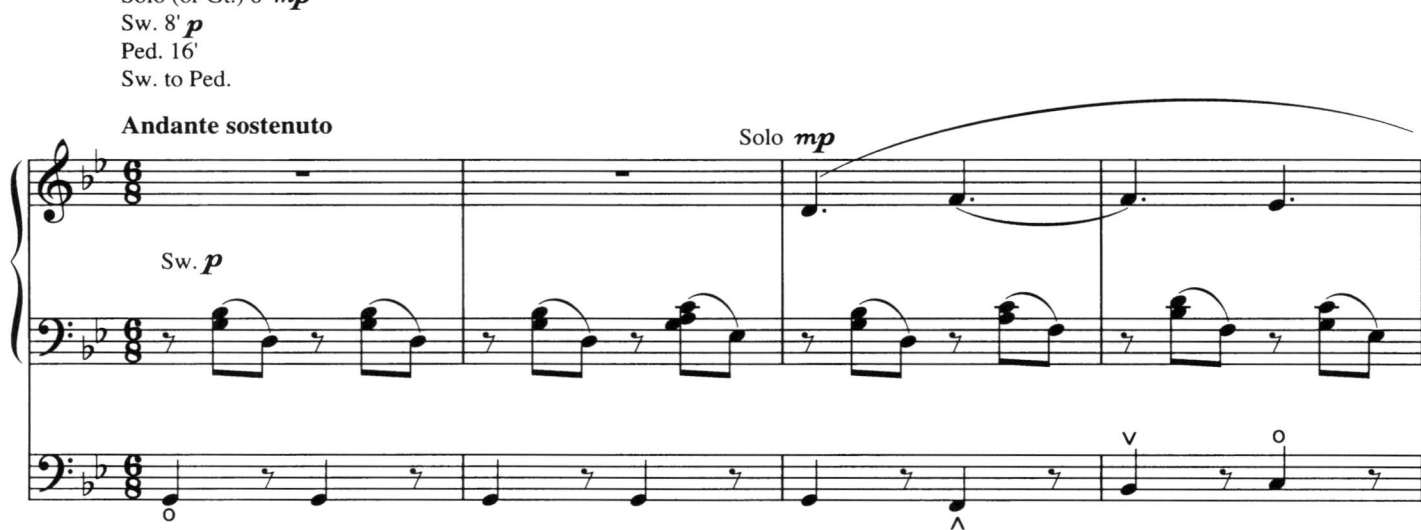

© Copyright 1999 Kevin Mayhew Ltd.
It is illegal to photocopy music.

DANCE OF THE BLESSED SPIRITS from 'ORPHEUS'

Christoph von Gluck (1714-1787)

© Copyright 1999 Kevin Mayhew Ltd.
It is illegal to photocopy music.

* 'Pivot' right heel on E without depressing it.